Published by Concordia Publishing House
3558 S. Jefferson Avenue, St. Louis, MO 63118-3968
1-800-325-3040 • www.cph.org

Text copyright © 2006 by Charles Lehmann
Illustrations copyright © 2006 Concordia Publishing House

Manufactured in China.

1 2 3 4 5 6 7 8 9   14 13 12 11 10 09 08 07 06

THE STORY OF CREATION

GOD
Made It for
YOU!

Written by CHARLES LEHMANN

Illustrated by KATHLEEN KEMLY

CONCORDIA PUBLISHING HOUSE · SAINT LOUIS

In the beginning, it was very dark.

No sun kept things warm. No moon made things bright.

No stars shone in the sky.

There were no light bulbs, no candles, no campfires.

There was no blinking, no twinkling, no flashing.

There was only God.

So God said, "Let there be light."

And there was light. It was bright everywhere.

All the darkness was gone.

God wanted there to be a time for darkness and a time for light.

So He separated the light from the darkness.

The light He called **day**. The darkness He called **night**.

It got dark in the evening, and it got bright in the morning.

God saw the light, and He liked it. He knew it was good.

On the **first day** God made light.

He made it for you!

Then God made the sky, blue and bright.

He also made the water, deep and wet.

The sky was beautiful, but no birds flew in it.

The water went on and on, but no fish swam in it.

God saw the water and the sky, and He liked them.

He knew they were good.

On the second day God made the water and the sky.

He made them for you!

Then God said, "Let the water come together in one place,

and let dry ground appear!" And it was so!

The waters came together in one place and dry ground appeared.

God made hills and valleys. He made mountains and plains.

God called the waters seas. The dry ground He called land.

God said, "Let there be pine trees, apple trees, watermelons, and bananas.

Let there be grass, bushes, dandelions, and daisies.

Let there be lots of plants that have seeds." And it was so!

The land turned **green**. Wonderful things grew in the ground.

Grass to walk on. Bushes to hide in. Dandelions to blow in the wind.

All kinds of wonderful **plants** everywhere.

God saw the land, the sea, and the plants, and **He liked them**.

He knew they were good.

On the **third day** God made the land, the sea, and the plants.

He made them for you!

Then God said,
"Let there be lights in the sky!

Big ones and little ones. Bright ones and dim ones. Let there be the **sun** and the **moon**, planets and stars."

So God made the sun to warm the day, and He made the moon to brighten the night. Planets and stars filled the sky. Big ones and little ones. Bright ones and dim ones.

Suddenly the night was as **beautiful** as the day. God saw the lights in the sky, and He liked them. He knew they were good.

On the **fourth day** God made the sun, the moon, and the stars. He made them for you!

Then God said, "Let the water be filled with all kinds of things that swim! Swordfish and dolphins. Whales and cod."

And it was so. God made the swordfish and dolphins, the whales and the cod. They swam and they played. The ocean was filled with many kinds of fish.

And God said, "Let the sky be full of all kinds of birds! Eagles and hawks, sparrows and doves."

And it was so. God made eagles and hawks, sparrows and doves. They chirped songs of joy to God, and music was born.

God saw the creatures in the sea and the air, and He liked them. He knew they were good.

On the fifth day God made fish and birds.
He made them for you!

Then God said, "Let the land be filled with all kinds of animals! Dogs and cats, sheep and cows, bears and giraffes."

So God created all kinds of animals to live on the land. Dogs and cats. Sheep and cows. Bears and giraffes. They ran and they jumped.

They ate and they played.

God looked at all He had made, and He liked it.

He knew it was good.

On the **sixth day** God made **animals.**

He made them for you!

God saw the **wonderful world** He had made. He looked at the flying birds, the barking dogs, the swimming whales, and the rolling hills. But something was missing.

So God said, "**Let us make man in our image** and let him take care of the fish of the sea, the birds of the air, and everything that moves on the ground!"

God took dirt from the ground and shaped it into a **man**. He put the man in a garden called Eden and He breathed into his nose the breath of life. **God named the man Adam.**

Adam looked at the wonderful world God had made and was excited by all the wonderful animals. There were big ones and little ones, red, blue, yellow, and green ones. But even when Adam gave names to all the animals, he couldn't find one to be his friend.

God said, "It is not good for the man to be alone."

So God made the man fall asleep, and He took part of Adam's side and made him a friend.

When Adam woke up, he saw the woman God had made and he loved her.
He named her Eve.

God saw all that He made. It was *very* good. He said to Adam and Eve,

"This week I made the whole world. I made it for you because I love you."

Then God said, "I will always take care of you.

You will have children, and I will love them too. Take care

of them, and teach them about Me."

On the sixth day, God made parents.
He made them for you!

The next day, the **seventh day**,
God rested from all the work He had done.

Everything God made was very good for a while.

But Adam and Eve disobeyed God.

They ate from the Tree of the Knowledge of Good and Evil

even after God had told them not to.

This made God sad and angry.

God had to punish them, so He made the man and the woman

leave the beautiful, perfect place He had made.

Adam and Eve and all the people born after them have sinned.

But God loved Adam and Eve and **He loves us too,**

so He promised He would make things better.

And that's just what He did!

God sent His Son, Jesus, to be a real person.

Jesus lived a perfect life for us and then He let Himself die in our place to take

the punishment for all our sin.

When Jesus died, God forgave me and you and Adam and Eve and everyone.

He forgave us for everything we do wrong. When God raised Jesus from the grave,

He showed us that He loves us and is still our Friend.

Jesus died on the cross to forgive our sins.

He did it for you!

A Note to Parents:

The story of creation is a beautiful image of God's love for us. Taking particular care, God made the universe in six days. In all He did, He was preparing a special place for us. As you talk with your child about this story, tell him how God made the world especially for him.

It is important for all children to know they are loved by God. When you are walking in a park, point to a tree. Say, "God made that for you!" When you buy a goldfish or a puppy, say, "God made it for you!"

Most important, remind your child that when God sent His Son, Jesus Christ, He sent Him for your child. Say to him, "God died on the cross. He did it for you!"

As your child grows older, use the Bible and other resources to teach about God's creation and our part in it. Help your child learn to say:

I believe that God has made me and all creatures; that He has given me my body and soul, eyes, ears, and all my members, my reason and all my senses, and still takes care of them.

He also gives me clothing and shoes, food and drink, house and home, wife and children, land, animals, and all I have. He richly and daily provides me with all that I need to support this body and life.

He defends me against all danger and guards and protects me from all evil.

All this He does out of fatherly, divine goodness and mercy, without any merit or worthiness in me. For all this it is my duty to thank and praise, serve and obey Him.

This is most certainly true.

The Author